25

285094

Burlingame, California
344-1164

———

1. **UNLESS OTHERWISE DESIGNATED,** books may
   be kept for two weeks and may be renewed once
   for the same length of time.

2. Overdue fees will be levied on all magazines, books,
   and phonograph record albums according to the
   schedule posted at the main desk.

3. **DAMAGES AND LOSSES** of Library-owned property
   will be paid for by the borrower.

4. **RESPONSIBILITY** for all books taken on his card
   rests with the borrower as well as for all fees ac-
   curing to his card. Notification of loss of card does
   not free the borrower of his responsibility.

5-13

stilts

stilts

BY
S. CARL HIRSCH

Illustrated by
Betty Fraser

The Viking Press   New York

FIRST EDITION

Copyright © 1972 by S. Carl Hirsch. All rights reserved

First published in 1972 by The Viking Press, Inc.

625 Madison Avenue, New York, N.Y. 10022

Published simultaneously in Canada

by The Macmillan Company of Canada Limited

Library of Congress catalog card number: 72-80512
Printed in U.S.A.

680   1. Stilts
      2. Games and toys
      3. Customs and folklore   SBN 670–67053–7

1 2 3 4 5 76 75 74 73 72

FOR SID AND MAE
Everlasting joy to you both
on your Marin mountain

the jest of the giants

The Archduke's mustache quivered with excitement. Astride his horse, he waited in the little Belgian village for the honor guard that was on its way to escort him into the nearby city of Namur.

A joke, a trick, a riddle? The Archduke loved them dearly. And there was a hint of all these in the mystery about the guardsmen. The Archduke chuckled, thinking about the letter from the governor.

The troop would arrive, the message said, "neither riding nor on foot." The Archduke, puzzling over the governor's words, had long since run out of guesses. There was nothing to do now but to wait until this strange honor guard made its appearance.

One of the Archduke's aides peered skyward. Despite the many new inventions in the year 1600, no one had yet equipped men with wings. Another aide was at the riverbank. Perhaps the Namur guardsmen would come swimming upstream like a school of well-trained fish?

At last there came a steady crunching beat, but it was not like the usual tramping of marching men. Suddenly an odd sight appeared through the morning mist.

It was an army of giants. In brilliant uniforms the splendid guardsmen flashed into full view — each one of them ten feet tall!

The Archduke could now see clearly that the company was "neither riding nor on foot." Each soldier was striding on a pair of tall stilts.

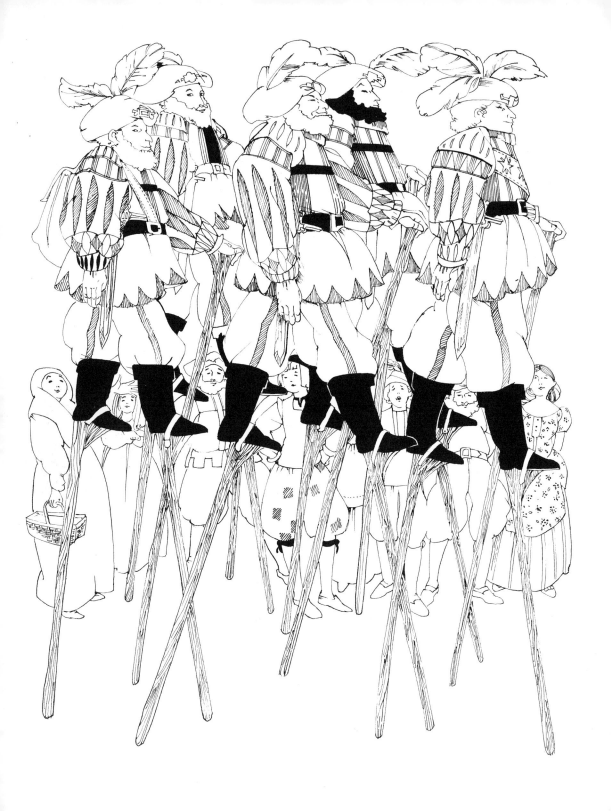

And so began a day of fun and feasting in Namur. The delighted Archduke was royally entertained. The visitor even tried out a pair of stilts, taking a few wobbling steps. Later that glorious spring evening, the Archduke raised his glass in a tribute to the city of Namur.

"To your wonderful guardsmen," was his toast to the townsfolk. "There are none in the world that can top them!"

tall tales

The story of stilts is full of strange surprises.
Who would expect to find fruit pickers on stilts
in the peach orchards of California?

And how curious it is to learn of stiltwalkers
in the folklore of ancient China. Or dancing to
the drumbeat of freedom in modern Africa. Or
striding through the history of America,
beginning far back in time.

In various countries, stilts are called walking
wood, knitting needles, chopsticks, and stalking
sticks.

Just when the first man took a stroll high on a
pair of wooden posts no one knows. But stilts
are part of legends from around the globe. And
stiltwalkers are clearly shown in decorations on
some ancient ruins.

Knowledge about stilts came to the New
World aboard the slave ships from Africa. In the
dark holds of those floating prisons were black
children who remembered the games and the
sports of their homelands. It was they who

taught other American children how to fashion a pair of poles into a delightful pastime.

Today a variety of factory-made stilts are on the market. But on any morning in any place where children live, the sound of the handsaw and the hammer may be heard briefly. And at once, a new breed of spindly creatures appears. These are the boys and girls who have suddenly come up in the world!

It takes no more than minutes to make a simple pair of stilts. But there are hours of enjoyment to follow.

The mastery of stilts begins with standing

just long enough to get started. Then one stumbles ahead, stiff-kneed and long-legged. At length, practice leads to a comfortable and confident stride. And finally there are stunts and races and games.

Stilts are for fun. But anyone who mounts a pair has suddenly climbed into a tradition that is as wide as the world and ages old.

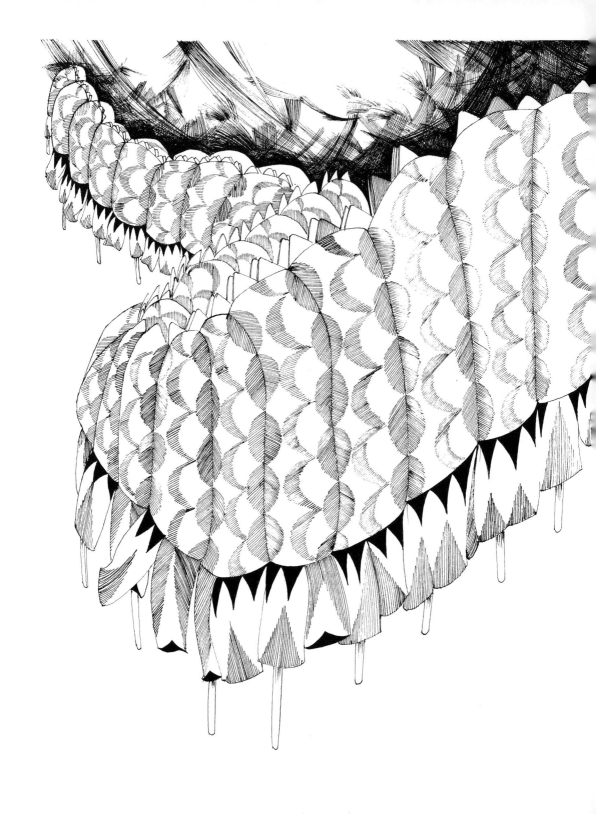

dragons, dancers, and devils

China's Liao River is an unruly stream that has often flooded its banks. The town of Newchwang owes its custom of stiltwalking to those days when the river water lay deep in its streets and covered the surrounding farms.

The Liao has since changed its course, leav-

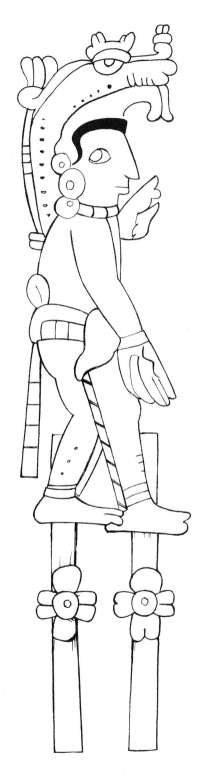

ing the town high and dry. But stilts are still among the traditions of Newchwang and remain dear to the hearts of its people.

Each New Year the town holds a pageant amid fireworks and lively music and colorful costumes. It is a parade on stilts. The main attraction is a twisting, rearing dragon, with its many long legs mounted on poles.

China's stiltwalkers go back thousands of years in time. Stilting is also an old tradition among people whose customs differ greatly from those of the Orient.

Men digging in the ruins of the great Benin civilization in what is now Nigeria recently found a large and beautiful plaque. It showed an African man in a long robe carrying a sword. He was mounted on stilts.

Half a world away in the Mexican state of Yucatán, some temple decorations of the ancient Mayan Indians were discovered only a few years ago. Clearly depicted were men on stilts who took part in religious ceremonies and dances. These stilt-dancers were supposed to bring good luck. Such rituals are still to be seen in the southern part of Mexico. Masked men dance for hours on four-foot stilts, performing according to ageless custom.

From the legends of ancient Rome come stories of street dancers on stilts who appealed to the gods. The dancers, dressed in costumes made of many-colored patches, were called *grallae* in Latin. The same word is used today as the scientific name for certain long-legged wading birds.

It is easy to understand why stilts were used especially in those rituals which celebrated the growing up of young people. In what is now Tanzania in East Africa, an old rite centered around a tribal dancer who was called the man in the treetop. Standing high on his stilts, he would pray that the young people of the tribe might grow tall and healthy and reach the very height of their ambitions.

Still another kind of religious ceremony has been carried on in the Central Provinces of India, where the shortage of food has long been a problem. A dance on stilts is performed each spring along with the sowing of seeds. The gods are asked to make the crops grow as tall as the stiltwalkers.

One of the oddest of folk tales about stilts comes from New Zealand. As do people everywhere, the Maoris sometimes lose things. Household items seem to disappear without a trace. To explain the mystery, people tell the fable of the thieving devils, who are pictured as going about stealthily on stilts. These mischief makers, it is said, reach into people's houses, snatch things, and vanish—without ever leaving a telltale footprint!

land of the stilt people

On the seacoast of southern France lies a soggy region called Les Landes. Changing seasonally from salt marsh to damp plain, much of it is neither land nor water.

For centuries its people found their own strange way to live with wetness. They relied on stilts.

Propped up on stilts, the shepherds tended their flocks. The mail carrier made his rounds, stumping on his stilts from dawn to sundown. Stiltwalking housewives, chatting in the market in their black clothes, were said to resemble large ravens perched on dead branches.

As for the children of Les Landes, they did their chores, went to school, carried on their play and sports—all on stilts. There were days when they hardly ever seemed to touch ground. No wonder they became the most skillful stiltwalkers in the world.

A young baker of Les Landes named Silvain Dornon even strode his way into fame. In the spring of 1891 Silvain set out on an odd journey. Towering on his stilts, he began walking eastward across France and beyond. He was an astonishing sight as he stalked through the villages, over the mountains, and across the farmlands of country after country. Silvain moved rapidly, taking great strides. He was out to make a record that no one has equalled to this day. The young baker ended his stiltwalking tour in Moscow fifty-eight days later, having covered a distance of more than two thousand miles!

tricks with sticks

Maybe it was children who first invented stilts. Certainly stilting has afforded young people play and pleasure in almost every country in the world. But stilts have been cleverly put to many practical uses by people of all ages as well.

For one thing, they offered a way to avoid cold, wet feet. In many a land stilts have sprouted suddenly in the rainy season. People have used them to ford swollen streams and to pass through flooded areas.

Such use is made of them still during the early spring in villages of southwestern Germany. The same idea occurred to the people of the Marquesas Islands in the South Pacific. During the period of heavy rains, stilts are the fashion.

In the Sudan the Ekoi people tell a story about a wise old man. He had been working on his little farm, planting yams. But the day was hot, and the ground was like a griddle, burning his bare feet. The old farmer sat under a tree and whittled a few branches. Soon he had some walking sticks on which he could carry out his planting in comfort. And it is said this was how the custom of wearing short stilts was begun in that sun-baked African land.

There are islands off Asia where, because of the ocean tides, the houses are built high above the ground. Some of these islanders have found a way to visit from one house to another without

endlessly climbing ladders. They move among these stilt houses on stilts of their own!

Many stories have come down to us about battles won and lost because of stilts. One such tale recounts how invading soldiers on stilts crossed a wide moat and stormed a British castle. Still another "tall story" of the past comes from Spain. It tells of a walled city, well protected from its enemies—until a clever commander attacked it with an army on stilts.

In modern times it is common to see a stilt-walker advertising some event or product or

service. Sometimes he appears high above the jam-packed city streets, carrying a sign or shouting his message or showering the crowd with handbills.

Recently the town of Pasadena, California, was getting ready for its annual Rose Bowl parade. As usual huge throngs gathered in the morning along the line of march. For anyone without a front row place, the chances of getting a good view of the parade were poor indeed.

One resident had an idea. He and his son went into their basement and spent a half hour with some woodworking tools.

At parade time the parents and children had a perfect view of the colorful floats, the marching bands, the entire flowery display. Standing on stilts, they watched the pageant over the heads of the crowd!

The view from a pair of high stilts may sometimes be a surprising one. At least it was to one stiltwalker, a circus clown.

no time to clown   One of the greatest clowns of all time was Ray Harris. He was the star-spangled performer in the giant circus that opened in San Diego in the spring of 1938.

Harris's specialty was high jinks on high stilts. But his biggest moment did not occur during a performance in the sawdust ring. It came between the acts and behind the scenes, as he was standing on his stilts in a narrow corridor that ran from the big top to the wild animal cages.

From his vantage point Harris could see that something was wrong. Just ahead, the plumed horses were acting strangely, snorting nervously and rearing on their haunches. The tension was being picked up by the herd of elephants just behind him, who were milling about, trumpeting in fear.

Suddenly a cry rang out—"Tiger escaped!" Harris looked down at the commotion. Men and animals had backed away from him in terror. Beneath him, between his stilts, was the giant striped cat, crouched and snarling!

The clown had to look twice before he remembered that it was his wooden legs and not

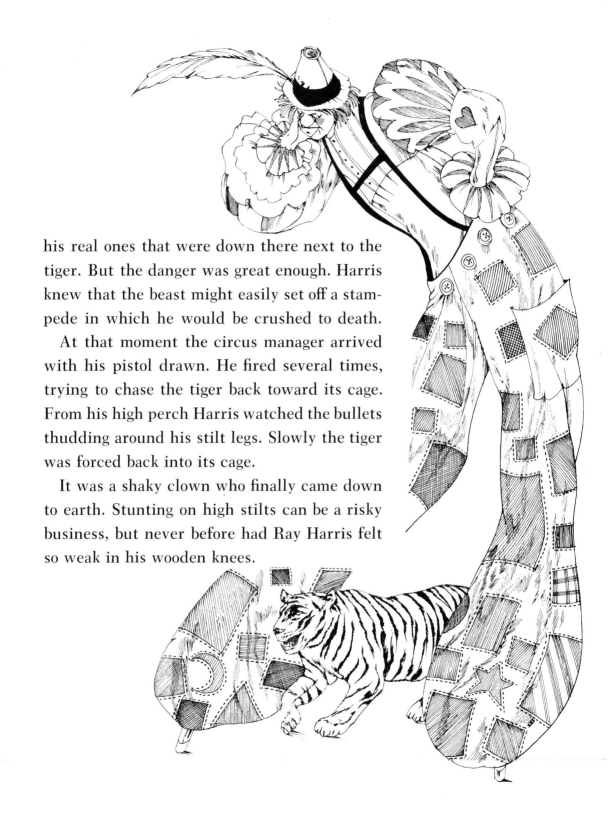

his real ones that were down there next to the tiger. But the danger was great enough. Harris knew that the beast might easily set off a stampede in which he would be crushed to death.

At that moment the circus manager arrived with his pistol drawn. He fired several times, trying to chase the tiger back toward its cage. From his high perch Harris watched the bullets thudding around his stilt legs. Slowly the tiger was forced back into its cage.

It was a shaky clown who finally came down to earth. Stunting on high stilts can be a risky business, but never before had Ray Harris felt so weak in his wooden knees.

leading the parade

Circus—the very word brings a tickle and a tingle. It is a thrilling, whirling, soaring world where the air seems filled with performers shot from cannons and acrobats on horseback, tightropes, and on the flying trapeze.

No circus would be complete without its stilt act. The high-stepping clowns bring endless wonder and merriment. And some circuses even feature bears and chimps performing on stilts.

An all-time favorite circus act begins with the ringmaster's ballyhoo of "the tallest man in the world!" Through the silver curtain steps—a midget. Behind him comes a normal-sized clown. Then another, on short stilts. A performer on high stilts follows. And last of all, leaving the audience gasping, comes the clown on super-stilts, strutting around at a dizzy altitude. He chats up there with the performers on the high swings, throws peanuts down on the audience,

and evades a motorcycle by letting it go between his legs.

Mr. Highpockets, a familiar type of long-legged clown, may be found where the fun is. He is at the carnival and the county fair. He is seen at Halloween. He leads the Thanksgiving Day parade that opens the holiday season in New York City. And he is there at the Mardi Gras in New Orleans. Often he is wearing an Uncle Sam suit, his striped, baggy breeches flapping around his skinny legs. However, this kind of comic also shows up at festivals and fun shows all over the world, from Rome to Tokyo and from Bombay to Buenos Aires.

The stiltwalker may even appear in a play of William Shakespeare. A recent production of *A Midsummer Night's Dream* featured the humorous character Bottom going through his pranks on stilts.

The earliest circuses were staged in the ancient towns along the Mediterranean Sea. A kind of Pied Piper on stilts can still be seen in some Italian ports leading the children of the town to a plaza where a small traveling circus puts on its lively show.

One famous big-top performer lives in London near Piccadilly Circus, which is not a circus at all but a busy circular area in the heart of the city. Harry Yelding claims to hold the world's record as the master of the tallest stilts of all.

This clown performs on a pair that measures twenty-two feet from his ankles to the ground. Yelding sometimes strolls through the London streets, window-shopping in third-story windows.

walking   ladders

In the fruit orchards of California they have a saying, "One pair of stilts is worth a dozen ladders."

That's why stilts are commonly used by growers of peaches, plums, and apricots. On aluminum stilts, these fruit farmers can prune and harvest their trees in the most handy manner.

Often these are triple stilts, each one made of three aluminum poles joined together like a three-legged stool. Two long poles are strapped to the sides of the leg just below the knee. The third piece is shorter and extends from the underside of the footrest to the ground. When the farmer mounts his walking ladders, every part of the tree is within his reach.

A few years ago in Phoenix, Arizona, a group of workmen arrived at the construction site of a large new shopping center. Somebody had forgotten to bring the ladders and scaffolding which were to be used in lathing and plastering the interior walls. The workers waited by idly until one of them, Bob Skaggs, had an idea.

Skaggs rummaged in a scrap woodpile. With the aid of saw, hammer, and nails, he quickly put together several pairs of stilts. Soon the workmen were lumbering along the building walls, busily carrying on their jobs. For Skaggs this was the beginning of a new line of work. He opened a factory supplying bricklayers, carpenters, electricians, painters, and plasterers with aluminum stilts.

The methods may be new, but the idea is an

old one. Stilts have long been used on jobs where the workers are required to move around at a high, fixed level. In Europe, where many houses still have thatched roofs, they are kept in repair by men on stilts.

Hops, which are flowers used in brewing beer, grow on vinelike plants twenty feet tall. In England, hop pickers harvesting the flowers on high stilts are a familiar sight.

In Toronto, Canada, there is a large factory where outdoor window washing is done on stilts. Recently a magazine article showed an agile Virginia housewife using stilts to help her do her spring housecleaning. And in southern France, an artist has been at work for years decorating the inside of a chapel—painting while on stilts. These are all people keeping up —high up—with their jobs.

For some people, stilts are a way of employment. For others, stilts are a way of enjoyment.

play's the thing

Walking wood is the name for the stilts used by some American Indian boys and girls.

Among western tribes, the young people let nature make their stilts for them. They simply select a straight sapling that has a strong fork or branch. This fork is cut off short in such a way that it becomes a natural, integral footrest.

In many countries the typical children's games are similar. As in America, young people everywhere have their own versions of tag, blindman's buff, hopscotch, and king of the hill. Sometimes children find ways of making these ordinary games more exciting. One way is to play them on stilts.

In the South Pacific, island people still tell of stilt races that were enjoyed in the old days. Boys and girls of all ages ran like large storks along the beaches. On festival days stilt races were spirited events, and the winners were honored with prizes.

On the island of Tahiti, the games sometimes get rough, although a referee stands by to see that there is fair play. Each player kicks with his stilt at a stilt of his opponent, trying to bring him to earth. Sometimes a kicker, aiming badly, succeeds only in throwing himself off balance and losing the game.

In Nigeria, it is usually the boys who are on stilts, trying to outdo each other in their stunts. They hop on one stilt, vie to outreach each other, and compete in their skill at stilting with no hands.

Play on stilts sometimes mimics the creatures seen in nature—the daddy longlegs spider, the tall wading birds, the giraffe.

The joy of stilts is mostly in simple play, in letting your mind tell its own tall tales as the stilts carry you along with your head in the clouds.

A Chinese poet, Li Po, recounting the childhood of a merchant's wife, wrote

I was then a little girl
With hair cut straight across my brow,
Playing on the garden fence,
And reaching toward a fruit tree bough,
When you rode by on bamboo stilts,
And reined your tall steed, crying, "Whoa!"
You plucked the plums beyond my reach,
In Chokan village long ago.

the bamboo horse

It is common to see Japanese boys and girls walking through newly fallen snow on their bamboo stilts. There are special bamboo horse games which are played only in the winter months. Other games are for the season of heavy rains, when only the most skillful young stilters manage to stay up out of the puddles.

Sometimes there is a contest to see who can take the longest step. This game is more tricky than it sounds. Frequently a player will over-step himself, tumble, and find himself rolling in the snow or mud.

Since it is all in fun, play on stilts is a delight-ful sport for the Japanese during the years they are growing up. Adults often speak of a close childhood companion in these words: "He was a friend of my bamboo horse."

Few areas of the world offer such quick and easy means for making stilts. Because Japan has many bamboo groves, a pair of poles may be selected of just the right length and thickness. Such poles are strong, and smooth to handle.

To make the footrests, Japanese children have learned the skill of tying on short bamboo crosspieces with thongs.

In America, stilts may be bought in almost any toy or sporting goods store. But many boys and girls want the joy of making their own. And if parents want to help, let them share the fun.

make your own

Stilts are quick and easy to make. There is no *one* right way to go about it. After you've made your first pair, you may want to experiment with another method.

First prepare the uprights. These may be wooden poles, the kind that are called one-by-twos or furring strips in the lumber yard. Begin with poles about seven feet long. To avoid splinters, the uprights need to be smooth. A little filing and planing, followed by sandpapering, should take care of that problem.

Another material that may be used for the upright poles is aluminum conduit, available from an electrical supply store.

Several kinds of rubber pads may be affixed to the bottoms of the uprights for better traction.

rubber pads

7'

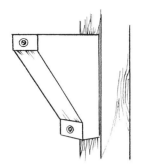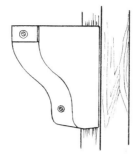

The footrests come next. These can be made out of scraps of one-inch lumber, three and one-half or four inches wide. They should be about six inches long. They can be triangular or cut away in a curving design (see above illustration).

In fastening the footrests to the uprights, you will first have to decide how high off the ground they should be. Judge for yourself, but don't try to reach the moon just yet!

The important thing is to mount the footrests securely to the uprights. This can be done in several ways. One method is to drill two holes through each footrest and matching holes through each upright. Then use two bolts and two nuts on each stilt. Another way is to use one bolt and one nut together with one long wood screw and washer for each footrest.

Ordinary angle irons may be useful in the construction.

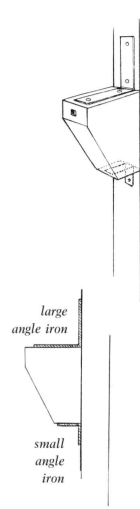

large angle iron

small angle iron

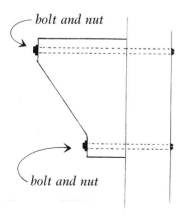

bolt and nut

bolt and nut

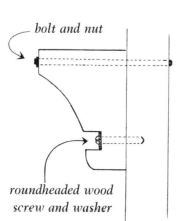

bolt and nut

roundheaded wood screw and washer

You will soon outgrow your first pair of stilts and may want to pass them on to someone else. That will be a good time to do some inventing on your own.

For example, the upright may be made of two pieces fastened together. This method has two advantages: it provides a shelf on which to mount the footrest; and it allows you to walk with the stilt leg more directly under your foot.

You may want to add straps to hold your feet securely to the footrests. You will find that these will permit you to raise each stilt with your foot as you walk. The straps can be made of leather, canvas belting, heavy rubber, or plastic. Use wood screws and washers to fasten straps to stilt and footrest.

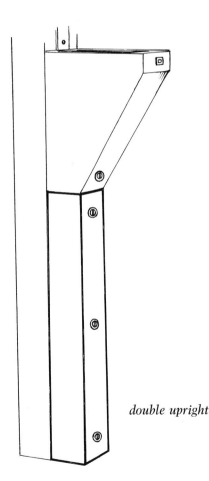

double upright

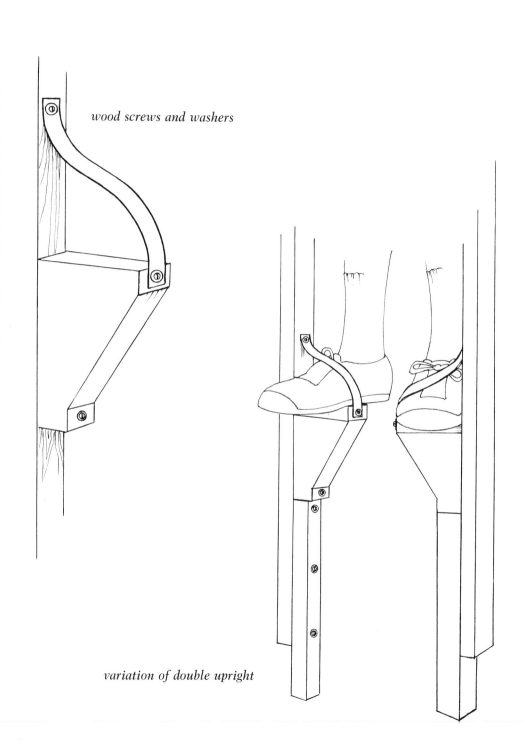

wood screws and washers

variation of double upright

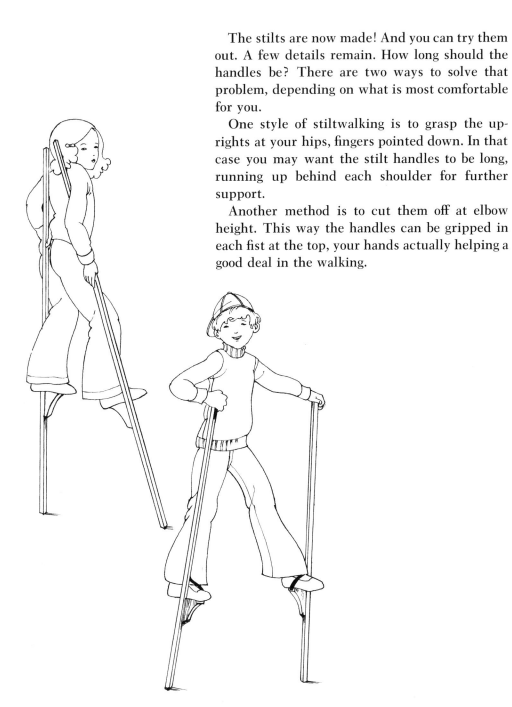

The stilts are now made! And you can try them out. A few details remain. How long should the handles be? There are two ways to solve that problem, depending on what is most comfortable for you.

One style of stiltwalking is to grasp the uprights at your hips, fingers pointed down. In that case you may want the stilt handles to be long, running up behind each shoulder for further support.

Another method is to cut them off at elbow height. This way the handles can be gripped in each fist at the top, your hands actually helping a good deal in the walking.

For the bold ones, hip stilts are the next challenge. These leave the hands free. In making this type, used by circus clowns, the uprights are cut off just above the waist. Belts strap the stilts firmly at the waist, below the knee, and at the ankle. A solid platform footrest may be made in the manner illustrated.

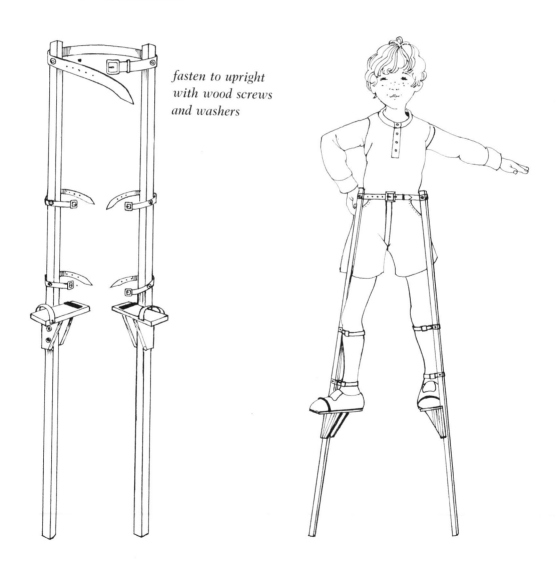

*fasten to upright
with wood screws
and washers*

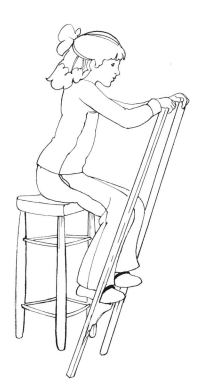

Don't hesitate to use balancing aids in beginning your stilting or in moving up to newer and higher stilt lengths. Start out your walking from a chair or box. In extending your skills, use a long balancing pole for added support.

There is some danger in stilting. A splinter, maybe. A bruise, perhaps. The best of the stilt-walkers have taken a tumble or two. And the taller they reach, the harder they fall.

It's all a matter of balance and a bit of practice. Stilts need to be mounted and handled carefully until you get the feel of them.

For a moment, stand up high. Step out—first one leg, then the other. Got the idea? Now stride out to glory!

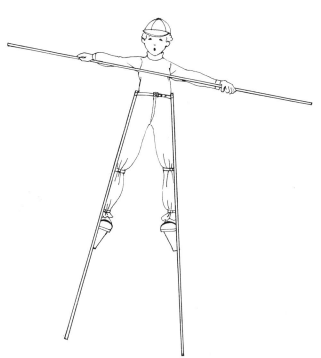